ETHICS OF POLITICS

Political Systems

Scott Witmer

Heinemann
LIBRARY
Chicago, Illinois

www.capstonepub.com
Visit our website to find out more information about Heinemann-Raintree books.

To order:
☎ Phone 800-747-4992
🖥 Visit www.capstonepub.com to browse our catalog and order online.

© 2013 Heinemann Library
an imprint of Capstone Global Library, LLC
Chicago, Illinois

Edited by Adam Miller, Louise Galpine, and Adrian Vigliano
Designed by Marcus Bell
Original illustrations © Capstone Global Library Ltd.
Illustrated by Darren Lingard
Picture research by Tracy Cummins
Production by Alison Parsons
Originated by Capstone Global Library Ltd.
Printed and bound in China by Leo Paper Products Ltd.

16 15 14 13 12
10 9 8 7 6 5 4 3 2 1

Library of Congress Cataloging-in-Publication Data
Witmer, Scott.
  Political systems / Scott Witmer.
    p. cm.—(Ethics of politics)
  Includes bibliographical references and index.
  ISBN 978-1-4329-6551-8 (hbk.)—ISBN 978-1-4329-6556-3 (pbk.) 1. Comparative government—Juvenile literature. I. Title.
  JF127.W57 2012
  320.3—dc23   2011043989

Acknowledgments
The author and publishers are grateful to the following for permission to reproduce copyright material: Alamy p. 33 (© Mary Evans Picture Library); Corbis pp. 13 (© Bettmann), 15 (© Corbis), 25 (© CHRISTIAN HARTMANN/Reuters); Getty Images pp. 5 (MOHAMMED ABED/AFP), 11 (MAHMUD TURKIA/AFP), 16 (SUHAIB SALEM/AFP), 20 (Getty Images/Universal Images Group), 23 (GIANLUIGI GUERCIA/AFP), 31 (Time Life Pictures/Mansell/Time Life Pictures), 34 (GOH CHAI HIN/AFP), 36 (FPG), 39 (Galerie Bilderwelt), 41 (AFP PHOTO), 43 (ODD ANDERSEN/AFP), 45 (BEHROUZ MEHRI/AFP), 46 (LIBOR HAJSKY/AFP), 49 (EMMANUEL DUNAND/AFP), 50 (NICHOLAS RATZENBOECK/AFP), 53 (d Jose Cabezas/AFP), 55 (Universal History Archive); istockphoto p. 29 (© Liz Leyden); Library of Congress Prints and Photographs Division p. 27; Shutterstock pp. 7 (© The Crow), 8 (© Georgios Kollidas), 19 (© 1000 Words).

Cover photograph of Egyptian health workers at Cairo's Tahrir Square reproduced with the permission of Getty Images (PEDRO UGARTE/AFP).

We would like to thank Jonathan Lipman for his invaluable help in the preparation of this book.

Every effort has been made to contact copyright holders of any material reproduced in this book. Any omissions will be rectified in subsequent printings if notice is given to the publisher.

CONTENTS

Some words are printed in bold, **like this**. You can find out what they mean by looking in the glossary.

THE ARAB SPRING REVOLT

It all began when a man set himself on fire.

It happened on the morning of December 17, 2010, in Sidi Bouzid. This town is in the country of Tunisia, in North Africa. As usual, 26-year-old Mohammed Bouazizi was selling fruit from his produce cart. A city official stopped him and took his scale. She told him he could not sell fruit without a license. Bouazizi knew he would have to pay money—a bribe—to get his scale back. But this time the official also slapped his face when he complained.

Bouazizi felt humiliated. He was also fed up with the **corruption** that made everyday life difficult for many Tunisians. So, he made a drastic decision that would echo throughout the world. Standing in the middle of traffic outside the office building of the city government, he poured gasoline over himself. As he lit a match, he shouted, "How do you expect me to make a living?" On January 4, Bouazizi died from his burns.[1]

Many Tunisians identified with the young man's anger. Zine Ben Ali, the **dictator** of Tunisia, had thrived for 23 years on the type of corruption that pushed Bouazizi over the edge. Agents of Ben Ali's **regime** would often throw critics into prison. Protesting was illegal.

But Bouazizi's dramatic example inspired many Tunisians to confront the desperate situation. Using social networking technology such as Facebook, thousands of people organized and marched through cities and towns across Tunisia. Hundreds were killed when Ben Ali ordered police to shoot his own people. But the violence only intensified their anger. Tens of thousands of people shut down the capital city, Tunis, in a mass protest. On January 14, Ben Ali fled the country.[2]

The wave of revolution

Following the success of the uprising in Tunisia, uprisings spread throughout the **Arab** world, in the Middle East and North Africa. Protests flared up in Yemen, Iran, Libya, Bahrain, Morocco, and Syria. Demonstrators demanded change in many countries where the people suffered as a result of lack of freedoms, government corruption, high unemployment, and other problems.[3]

In Egypt, the spreading wave of revolution reached its peak. On February 11, 2011, after 18 straight days of nationwide protests, President Hosni Mubarak left office. The military took temporary control of the government. Egyptians had freed themselves from the corruption that had defined the previous 30 years of Mubarak's rule.[4]

The scene of wild celebration in Cairo's Tahrir Square in February 2011 marked the end of an era.

But what comes next? Will new governments be more open and fair? Or will a worse system of **politics** take the place of the dictators who are removed from power? What factors push people to demand **political** changes?

In this book, we will look at the **ethics** (the concepts of right and wrong) of different political systems. Through this process, we may learn why governments succeed or fail—and how they can be changed.

WHAT ARE POLITICAL SYSTEMS?

What do we mean by political systems? Essentially, politics is how human beings organize everyday social life. But people have many different ideas about how society should be organized. This leads to different political systems. Political systems are large-scale methods of social organization.

For example, consider something like roads, which everyone uses. Where should roads be built? Who should pay to build or maintain them? Who should build them? Some form of social organization is needed to propose ideas for such decisions—and to debate the best solutions.

Now think about the many different things society must organize: housing, public safety, transportation, employment, food, health care, and more. For every aspect of social life, there are **policies** that have been decided by some sort of political organization.

Politics must also address the ethics of human behavior. Laws are created as restrictions against unethical behavior like stealing or killing.

In this chapter, we will briefly examine some of the characteristics that all political systems share. To understand the basic features of political systems, it is best to start at the beginning. Where did political systems come from?

The roots of political systems

Political organization first began with the earliest civilizations, around 6,000 years ago. People first settled in river valleys where they could grow crops and raise livestock. Over time, disorganized communities developed into ordered societies.

Like all areas of ancient social life, politics were a part of religion. **Ethical** rules and laws were justified by religious beliefs about how people should behave toward one another. Political leaders were seen as representatives of the gods.

Under the direction of leaders, large-scale social projects, such as irrigation (bringing water to where it is needed), allowed early societies to thrive and grow. Leaders could also organize people to fight against enemies.[1]

These early communities were known as tribes. Members of a tribe shared values, religious beliefs, a language, and customs. (These tribes still exist today in the form of **ethnic** groups, also known as **nations**, that share common traditions.) As early settlements grew, people from different tribes with different customs came together. They did not always get along. Standards of law and authority became necessary to keep order. Rules were imposed to regulate behavior and ensure survival.[2]

The basic functions of political systems were there from the start: protection, order, and the organization and development of resources like water. Thus, at a basic level most political systems have always tried to meet these human needs.

Plato (depicted in this statue) was a great thinker from ancient Greece. He and his student Aristotle set down many ideas about how political organizations should function.

Freedom from politics?

Are politics necessary for human social life? Do people have the **right** to live their lives without concerning themselves with the problems of political and social organization?

As nations grew, they formed **states**. In modern terms, states are independent geographic territories. Many people identify the government of a state with the state itself—even though a state may have many different governments over time.

Governments are organized **institutions** with the power and authority to control social behaviors. They also have the ability to use force to protect (or restrict) the **civilian** population.[3] From an ethical perspective, governments are responsible for enforcing laws. The laws of governments maintain a sense of right and wrong in society. But they also limit citizens' freedoms.

Ideology and aspirations

Political systems are not just the institutions of government. They are also the ideas, or **ideologies**, that define and shape a government. An ideology is a set of ideas that defines the values of a political system.

Political change often starts as a rejection of existing conditions. It is also the result of new political ideologies that develop over time and challenge existing ideologies. But how are political ideologies formed in the first place?[4]

Political ideologies result from different ideas about how social life should be organized to best meet everyone's needs. Much political thought grew out of the **Enlightenment**. This was a period of philosophical and cultural advancement in Europe that lasted from the mid-17th to the 18th centuries. Enlightenment thinkers used reason to examine political power. They were especially concerned with the idea of rights, or ethical guarantees, such as freedom.

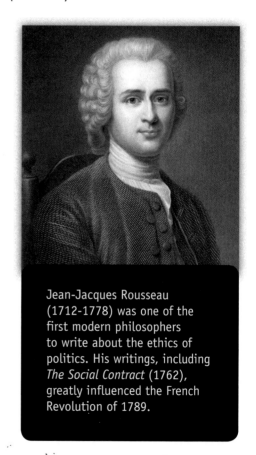

Jean-Jacques Rousseau (1712-1778) was one of the first modern philosophers to write about the ethics of politics. His writings, including *The Social Contract* (1762), greatly influenced the French Revolution of 1789.

In the 17th century, philosophers such as Englishman Thomas Hobbes began to question the limits of state power. Hobbes argued that the power of the government should be balanced by individual rights. He questioned what justifies the unlimited power of the state. When the state has unlimited power, this helps create wealth and security. But it can also take away political and social freedoms from citizens.[5]

The emphasis on rights marked an important stage in humankind's attempt to analyze and shape political systems. It resulted in the foundation of political science. This is the study of political systems and human social behavior.

Political systems today

No political system exists in pure form. Instead, in the real world, governments represent political systems to varying degrees.

We can look at real-life governments as models. They can help us understand political systems in action. They can also help us understand the ethical potential of different forms of government. By learning from history, we can shape governments in a way that allows people to live securely and freely.

Modern governments serve a range of purposes beyond the basic functions of protection and order. Governments that no longer meet the needs of the population are often changed through **reform** (gradual political changes) or revolution. Sometimes governments can also be changed when outside governments choose to become involved.

Legitimate authority?

Who has the right to rule? Political **legitimacy** means that the people accept that the government's authority is justified. It is a defining factor of political systems. Many forms of rule that were once accepted as legitimate are no longer considered so today. For example, religion, heredity (rule by birthright), and military power are less likely to be considered legitimate bases of authority than they were even 100 years ago. What defines a legitimate form of government today?

AUTHORITARIANISM

As the 2011 Arab Spring uprisings spread through the Middle East and North Africa (see pages 4 and 5), the region's rulers worried about the growing threat of revolution.

Colonel Muammar el-Qaddafi, the leader of Libya, in North Africa, watched the neighboring dictators of Egypt and Tunisia topple under the wave of protests. Qaddafi was determined not to give up power without a fight.

What began as a **democratic** revolution in Libya soon erupted into a bloody civil war, meaning a war fought among people within the same country. Qaddafi's army attacked his own citizens with overwhelming force. The rebels faced such brutal violence from the government forces that the United States and the North Atlantic Treaty Organization (NATO), a group made up of the United States and European powers, undertook air strikes to prevent the rebels from being wiped out.[1]

In August 2011, after six months of civil war, Libyan rebels forced Qaddafi from power. But Qaddafi and those loyal to his regime continued to fight in scattered cities and towns. Qaddafi was finally captured and killed by rebel forces in his hometown of Surt on October 20. The civil war resulted in a violent end for the brutal ruler.

Power and violence

Qaddafi's violent response to the threat of political change was typical of regimes that hold total power. **Absolute power** is often based on the use or threat of violence. Most rulers in the Middle East and North Africa are **authoritarian**. This means they have total control over politics in their country. Authoritarian regimes often use harsh methods to maintain that power.

Authoritarian rulers may be known as dictators, emperors, or czars. They can come to power in a variety of ways. They may originally gain power by motivating the people through some sort of ideology. Or they may take power through a struggle against a previous authoritarian ruler or against the influence of a foreign power. However, once they achieve power, their political decisions are seldom guided by ideology. More often, their rule is determined by their personal beliefs and their own self-interest.[2]

In order to ensure their control, authoritarian rulers restrict or outlaw political debate or criticism. Their actions do not need the approval of their people. In fact, they often silence political critics by throwing them in jail.

Authoritarian rulers cannot be removed from office except by force. They may hold elections, which offer the illusion of political choice. But these elections typically do not result in actual political changes.[3] The ruling regime often rigs the election results by directly controlling the process by which votes are cast or counted. But even without direct control of elections, authoritarian regimes can still guarantee their success by controlling what gets reported in the press and suppressing the political opposition.

MUAMMAR EL-QADDAFI (1942–2011)

Muammar el-Qaddafi first came to power in 1969 by leading a military **coup** (a sudden action to take power) against Libya's King Idris. He was only 27 years old at the time. Qaddafi's rule was based on ideals of unity among Arabs, especially as resistance against the influence of Western countries.

For much of his career, Qaddafi was known for supporting international terrorism. He also made radical statements against Western governments. His regime was responsible for the 1988 bombing of Pan Am Flight 103 over Lockerbie, Scotland, that killed 270 people. In 2003, Qaddafi made gestures to restore relationships with the West, most notably by abandoning efforts to develop nuclear weapons. By the time he was driven from power by a popular uprising in 2011, he had ruled for 42 years, longer than any modern Arab or African leader. His death on October 20, 2011, ended a long and brutal reign.[4]

Muammar el-Qaddafi delivering a speech in June 2010.

Military rule

Military regimes, known as juntas, are among the most common forms of authoritarian rule.[5] Juntas gain power when military leaders overthrow existing governments. Sometimes these regimes remain in power—although they often do not last long. Most existing juntas, which are mainly in Africa, are less than 20 years old.

In some cases, military leaders step down to make way for a civilian government. In Ghana, in West Africa, for example, Jerry Rawlings led a military coup that overthrew the civilian government on December 31, 1981. Rawlings ruled as a military dictator until 1992, when he retired from the military and ran for president in democratic elections. He was elected to the presidency twice and held the office until 2000, when the constitution prevented him from seeking a third term.

Even after stepping aside for civilian rule, a military regime may return when it feels order needs to be restored. The military in Pakistan, in South Asia, for example, often asserts its political power.[6]

Human rights

Many authoritarian regimes have very poor human rights records.[7] Because they do not have to answer to their citizens, authoritarian rulers often do not hesitate to use brutal force. For example, the regime of Robert Mugabe in Zimbabwe, in southern Africa, has been frequently cited by human rights organizations for widespread torture and assault against political critics.

One of the most horrible examples of an authoritarian leader abusing power is Jean-Bédel Bokassa. He was emperor of the Central African **Republic** (later the Central African Empire) from 1966 to 1979. Bokassa personally participated in the murder of over 100 schoolchildren. The children had thrown rocks at his Rolls-Royce, protesting the fact that they had to buy expensive school uniforms from a factory owned by Bokassa's family. Bokassa was convicted of this crime in 1986, but he served only seven years in prison.[8]

However, there have also been examples of authoritarian rulers who have had positive effects on society. For example, Emperor Meiji of Japan modernized Japanese society according to Western standards and transformed Japan's military into a major world power. He ruled from 1867 until his death in 1912. There is always the potential for enlightened authoritarian rulers to rule ethically. Such rulers are rare, however. As British historian Lord Acton said, "Power tends to **corrupt**, and absolute power corrupts absolutely."[9]

Idi Amin Dada was a dictator of Uganda, in East Africa, from 1971 to 1979. Amin's brutal regime was responsible for up to half a million deaths.

AUGUSTO PINOCHET (1915–2006)

In 1973, General Augusto Pinochet Ugarte led a military coup in Chile, in South America, that removed the democratically elected president, Salvadore Allende. Pinochet quickly put in place extreme and brutal violence against supporters of the former government. In the first few months of his reign, up to 30,000 people who openly disagreed with him were killed. About 65,000 were thrown in jail without a trial. Pinochet's human rights abuses became known around the world.

In 1980, Pinochet approved a **constitution** that allowed democratic elections. He was voted out of office in 1989, but he remained head of the military. Although he was arrested by the United Kingdom in 1998 for his human rights abuses, he was never tried due to poor health. He died in 2006.[10]

Personal rule

Many dictators organize their governments through what is known as personal rule. That means that they surround themselves with a system of patrons (supporters who provide money), friends, family, and sometimes rivals.

This ensures that the people in these positions depend on the dictator and will support his decisions. It also means that people who fill the government posts are not necessarily the best suited for the job. For this reason, systems of personal rule are very unstable, corrupt, and unpredictable.[11] Haile Selassie was the emperor of Ethiopia, in the Horn of Africa, from 1930 to 1974. He was known to appoint unqualified officials—in order to make himself seem more politically skilled by comparison.

Theocratic rule

Theocracy is rule by religious authority. In modern times, theocracy has nearly disappeared. But there are examples of it.

In Iran, a 1978 revolution overthrew Muhammad Reza Shah Pahlavi. A range of political opponents led the protests that led to the revolution. These people were unhappy with the fact that the shah (leader) put his political critics in prison. His opponents also did not like the shah's **economic** policies.

The Islamic clergy (religious people) led by Ayatollah Khomeini quickly took control of the revolution. They began to enforce traditional Islamic values. They did so in reaction to what they saw as the corrupting cultural influence of the West.[12]

Today, Islam dominates government ideology in Iran. Sharia law (traditional Islamic law), ayatollahs (Muslim religious leaders), and religious scholars continue to guide government policy. However, the representative government in Iran serves as a balance to Islamic authority.[13]

Islam is also a significant factor as the state religion in other countries, including Saudi Arabia (in the Middle East) and Somalia (in the Horn of Africa). However, it has not influenced the political systems in those countries to the degree that it has in Iran.

Today, there are signs that theocracy may reemerge in the form of Islamic **nationalism**, which is political rule based on Islamic religious principles. The Taliban was the Islamic government of Afghanistan, in South and Central Asia, from 1996 to 2001. It is one recent example of this type of government.

In Pakistan, in regional tribal governments in places like Waziristan, Sharia law is followed. This often brings these regional authorities into conflict with the national government. Some strict Muslims in Pakistan want to turn the country into an Islamic state.[14]

Italian philosopher Niccolo Machiavelli (1469-1527) is best known for his book *The Prince*, in which he advises rulers to sometimes be ruthless and devious in order to maintain their hold on power.

Monarchy

Absolute power has its roots in **monarchy**, meaning the rule of kings. Monarchy is one of the oldest political systems, having developed from tribal communities. It was the major political system for thousands of years.

Kings were considered legitimate rulers by "divine right." This means they were seen either as a representative of God or as a protector of the faith. Kings claim this right through birth, known as hereditary lineage or dynasty.

Dynasties often first came to power through force, either by conquering foreign lands or by overthrowing a previous dynasty. Neighboring states often followed a different religion. This meant that a new religion would be imposed if the **monarch's** territory were conquered. In this way, monarchs were seen as defenders of their religion against threats from outside.

Balancing power

The power of monarchs in modern times is often limited by constitutions. For example, in the United Kingdom, although there is a monarch (Queen Elizabeth), the prime minister and **Parliament** actually run the government.

King Abdullah bin Abdul-Aziz of Saudi Arabia is one of the world's last remaining absolute monarchs. King Abdullah secures his power by maintaining a balance of tradition and reform.

Modern monarchs in democratic societies, such as the British queen and Japanese emperor, often hold a ceremonial role. Because they do not have to concern themselves with the running of the country, their time is free for charity and building relationships with other countries. They are also stable representatives of the state through times of political crisis. Elections may change the government, but monarchs can remain a symbol of national unity beyond the world of politics.

Today, most absolute monarchies are in the Middle East, including in Saudi Arabia, Qatar, and the United Arab Emirates. Many of these monarchies are wealthy because they are located in an oil-rich part of the world.[15] Middle Eastern kings (sometimes known as sultans or sheiks) are often balanced by religious authorities or other elements of government.

Is absolute power legitimate?

Absolute rule is sometimes considered a guarantee of order for unstable states. Some **political scientists** argue that strong one-party regimes can bring stability to areas that struggle with tribal, ethnic, and religious tensions.[16]

However, such regimes are rarely responsive to the needs of their citizens. Dictators govern in their own interest rather than the interests of their people. Absolute power also has great potential to become corrupted. Authoritarian regimes frequently resort to violence to silence their critics and keep their hold on power. This is why authoritarian regimes are often rejected by their own people in favor of a form of government chosen by the people.

Constitution in Morocco

When Arab Spring protests erupted in Morocco, in North Africa, in 2011, authoritarian ruler King Mohammad VI at first responded with violence. But faced with the continuing challenge to his rule, the king introduced constitutional reforms that granted more power to elected officials. By slowly adapting to a **constitutional monarchy**, King Mohammad VI maintained his rule, while calming the democratic demands of the protest movement.[17]

DEMOCRACY

The word **democracy** is often used in politics. But what does it mean?

The word comes from the Greek words *demos*, meaning "people," and *kratos*, meaning "rule." In other words, it means a form of government in which the people rule. Quite simply, democracy is a political system in which people decide how they are governed. This arrangement requires the political equality of all citizens.

Political scientists often interpret the concept of democracy differently. Some do not consider it an ideology or a political system. Rather, they view it as a decision-making process. Others define democracy as a set of institutions that guarantee political equality.

Political safeguards

Elections are perhaps the most important democratic institution. Because elections are held in cycles, government leaders must answer to voters. They can be voted out of office if people do not like their policies.

Democracies typically also include other legal safeguards against abuses of power.[1] One such safeguard is a constitution that guarantees and protects rights, while also defining the limits of state power.

Democratic governments are usually split up into several institutions. For example, in the United States, the government is divided into three branches: the executive branch (the president), the legislative branch (Congress), and the judicial branch (the Supreme Court). Each of these branches keeps the others from becoming too powerful. The United States further balances power through federalism. This is the division of power among states and a central national government.[2]

Another important function of democracies is political **pluralism**, or competing political views. Political competition helps ensure a diverse range of opinions over political issues. Open debate is often protected and encouraged by such factors as the right to free speech and to independent media such as newspapers.[3]

Thousands of Thailand's pro-democracy "red shirts" demonstrators hold a public protest in December 2010.

A democratic transition

Thailand has a constitutional monarchy. The country has been politically unstable for many years. A power struggle among royalists (those loyal to the monarchy), businesspeople, and military officers led to a series of coups that produced five prime ministers in as many years. In 2010, poor people led mass protests. They demanded new elections to replace the prime minister and parliament, since they had not taken power legitimately.

An election held in 2011 brought to power Yingluck Shinawatra, who became the country's first female prime minister. Her Pheu Thai Party, which represents the poor, also gained power. The landslide victory was seen as a rejection of a political system that excluded the poor—who make up most of Thailand's population. It is also a strong example of democracy in action.[4]

The spread of democracy

Today, democracy is the dominant political system. Most of the world's people live under some form of democratic government.[5]

Democracy originated in Europe, where most of the world's oldest stable democracies are located. But today it has spread to all parts of the world.[6] Democracy is so widespread that even nondemocratic governments claim to support democratic principles. This is because democracy is considered a legitimate form of government. Laws and policies seem justified when they are approved by the participation of free and equal citizens.[7]

But why is democracy seen as the most legitimate form of government? A quick look at history will provide some context.

Modern democracy can be traced to the two major democratic revolutions of the 18th century: the American Revolution (1775–83) and the French Revolution (1787–99). The American Declaration of Independence of 1776 cast off British **colonial** rule. It stated that men are born free with equal rights, and that the government is responsible for protecting these rights. It also emphasized that the people are the legitimate source of political authority. The French Revolution ended France's monarchy. It also advanced the concept of equality in political affairs.[8]

The famous painting *Liberty Leading the People* by Eugène Delacroix (1830) symbolizes the French Revolution's struggle for political freedom.

Classical models of democracy

As they formed the United States, North American colonists turned to ancient Greece for models of democracy.

In the 5th century BCE, Athens was the most prominent city-state in Greece. It was governed by direct democracy, in which citizens are directly involved in political decisions. In this type of government, there is no difference between state and society. The concept of being a citizen was linked with being active in government. Public affairs were valued over private life. Citizens were fulfilled through political participation.

However, the concept of who was considered a citizen was tightly restricted. It did not include women or slaves.[9] The Athenian model was also for a relatively small community. Its idea of direct democracy cannot be imitated on a large scale.[10]

The next major historical example was ancient Rome, which was similar to Athens. Rome was a republic, a form of government in which citizens choose the leader. The government of Rome also emphasized a sense of public duty. Although Rome was an **oligarchy** (governed by an elite group), Roman ideas of citizenship were highly influential for later democracies.[11]

SAN MARINO: THE WORLD'S OLDEST DEMOCRATIC REPUBLIC

The longest-surviving independent state in the world is a territory surrounded on all sides in Italy, known as the Most Serene Republic of San Marino. St. Marinus founded it in 301 CE as a small Christian community. In the 19th century, the 24-square-mile (61.2-square-kilometer) nation survived as a city-state after many other territories became unified as Italy.

San Marino's government is based on its "governing principles," a type of informal constitution framed in 1600. San Marino's small size and population (around 30,000 people) make it a unique form of democracy. Political decisions are made by citizens through a General Council of 60 members. In 1992, San Marino became the smallest member of the United Nations.[12]

The evolution of democratic ideology

The next stage of historical democracy did not occur until the early Renaissance, a period of cultural reform that lasted from the 14th to the 17th centuries in Europe. Here, democracy reemerged in the city-states of Italy. Political participation was still important. But Italian democracy emphasized the idea that the community was the highest source of authority. The highest political ideal was the freedom of citizens.

The democratic ideals of the Italian city-states were eventually taken over by the Christian **theocratic** authorities of the Middle Ages (a historical period in Europe lasting from about the 5th to the 15th centuries). It was not until the end of the 16th century, and the dawn of the European Enlightenment (see pages 8 and 9), that a reconsideration of democratic politics occurred.

The limits of political authority and the rights of man then became the focus of European political thought. The Protestant Reformation was a 16th-century reevaluation of Christian religious authority. It inspired new ways of thinking about obedience to political authority.[13] The concept that human beings are individuals with rights became an important factor in politics.[14]

In the 18th and early 19th centuries, political thinkers James Madison, Jeremy Bentham, and James Mill also contributed to the theory of democracy. Most importantly, they emphasized that political leaders should be held accountable to the governed through institutions such as voting and pluralism. These were seen as essential elements in the balance between authority and liberty.[15]

Citizenship for all

However, these theories did not yet address who would be considered a citizen. The role of citizen was restricted to white men who owned property. For centuries, voting rights were denied to many groups. Through their struggles for the right to vote, women, the working classes, and nonwhites were eventually able to attain equality.

Ethical responsibility

Do citizens have a responsibility to be involved in their government? Is the right to vote an obligation? By leaving political decisions to others, are you risking your rights as a citizen?

As recently as the 20th century, African Americans still did not have adequate voting protections. It was not until the civil rights movement of the 1950s and 1960s that they achieved full equality at the voting booth. Black Africans in South Africa were also denied political equality from 1948 to 1994. This happened under the racial segregation policy of apartheid, which created separate societies for whites and blacks. Today, it is widely accepted that citizenship rights should apply equally to all adults.[16]

Supporters of South Africa's ruling party, the African National Congress, demonstrate in Cape Town in 2007. Under the policy of apartheid, black South Africans were denied voting rights until 1994.

Representative democracy

Today, representative democratic governments are found in the United States, the United Kingdom, Germany, Japan, Australia, South Africa, Costa Rica, and other places throughout the world.[17] In representative democracy, elected officials represent the interests of citizens. Political decisions are the responsibility of those who are elected. Elected bodies may take the form of congresses, parliaments, or other groups.

Citizens of classical democracies would probably not recognize democracy in its modern form. The lack of opportunity for direct involvement in political life by all citizens—not just representatives—would seem undemocratic.

The value of political debate

In the 20th century, many states expressed their independence from colonial or authoritarian rule. They often achieved this through democratic means. Representative government, equal rights, and free elections are common elements of many states with new governments.

New democracies, such as those in Latin America and the former Soviet Union (see pages 38 and 39), often struggle with the examples set by earlier, undemocratic regimes. Often, stable democracies can only develop in countries with some history of democratic organization. This is a difficult thing to achieve under **repressive** regimes that do not allow political debate.[18]

Today, elected officials represent political parties that include a wide range of interests. Within democratic systems, a wide range of political viewpoints allows ideologies to compete. The political extremes are often defined as liberal and conservative. These terms have different meanings in different countries according to the political traditions of that government.

A DIVIDED OPPOSITION

In Myanmar, in Southeast Asia, pro-democracy leader Daw Aung San Suu Kyi was put under house arrest on and off for a total of 15 years. The military-backed government had wanted to remove her as a threat, as part of its crackdown on democracy activists. She won the Nobel Peace Price for her efforts. She was finally released in November 2010, after Myanmar's first election in 20 years.

Aung San Suu Kyi's party, the National League, had won an election back in 1990. However, the ruling generals did not respect the results. So, in 2010 Aung San Suu Kyi directed her party not to participate in the election, as she did not consider it fair or democratic. Some party members disagreed with this approach. They formed their own party to run in the election. This shows that democratic movements must often make difficult decisions about how to challenge nondemocratic regimes.[19]

Democratic politics are often associated with argument and dispute. Politicians must constantly debate their ideas with political opponents. Often political disagreements can become angry or bitter. Democracy is in many ways a continuous struggle, in which questions of authority and rights are constantly challenged.[20]

Swiss political leaders prepare to debate on live television in 2008.

The world's largest democracy

It is easy to have democracy in an area the size of a town, where everyone can be involved directly in the political process. But how does democracy work on a large scale?

India is the world's largest democracy, with a population of over one billion people. The government is run by two houses of parliament. The House of the State is elected by legislatures (law-making bodies) of the 28 states. The 545-seat House of the People is made up of a group of over a dozen political parties elected directly. Members of the House of the People elect a prime minister, who is in charge of the government. In addition to the state legislatures, the constitution provides for a supreme court, which has the authority to judge the laws passed by parliament.[21]

ECONOMIC ALTERNATIVES

Economics has always been a factor in politics. But the connection between economics and politics became even stronger during the Industrial Revolution, a period of rapid technological change that began in Britain around 1750.

The development of the steam engine during the 18th century made it possible for machines to quickly do work that had previously been done by hand. Factories used large-scale machine production to create textiles (cloth) and other products. This mode of production led to large profits for factory owners. They made more money than had ever been possible before. But the drive for profit had many side effects.[1]

The industrial transformation

Rapid economic growth transformed society. Workers moved away from villages and farms to live near the factories in which they worked. Cities became the economic centers of production. Along with cities, transportation and communication technology also expanded during the Industrial Revolution.

But working conditions in industrial factories were extremely unhealthy and dangerous. Because the technology was new, there were no standards of safety. People were often injured as a result of the pressure to increase production. Fast-moving assembly-line machines would occasionally cut off fingers or limbs. Young children often had to work to support their family. Factories were also quite dirty, forcing workers to breathe polluted air.

Work began to shape social life in a way that it had not done before. People worked long, set hours at boring, repetitive tasks for very little money. The social cost of economic progress began to inspire resentment among the workers, as they struggled in poverty while their bosses grew rich.

Conflict between the owners of production and the workers contributed a new dimension to political struggle. Political thinkers began to focus not just on political organization, but also on economic conditions. The clash between the values of the competing economic systems of **capitalism** (see pages 28 and 29) and **socialism** (see pages 30 and 31) gained momentum throughout the 19th century.[2]

What do you think?

Is economics a political issue? Should politicians decide how businesses operate and how wealth is distributed in society? Should the government regulate such things as terms of employment, workplace safety, and the environmental effects of industry?

During the Industrial Revolution, mills like this textile spinning room in Cherryville, North Carolina (shown here in 1908), made work faster and more profitable, but also more dangerous and repetitive.

Capitalism

Capitalism is a system of economic organization. It is based on the production of goods for a personal profit. In a **capitalist** system, resources such as land, the machines of industry, and even ideas for products or services are considered private property.

Capitalist economies also include legal institutions. These guarantee to the owners of the means of production, such as factories, that they will keep whatever profits they make—minus taxes claimed by the government. Another important element of capitalism is growth. Profit is continuously created through cycles of investment, credit, and more.[3]

Features of capitalistic activity such as money and markets where goods are exchanged have been around for over 500 years. Capitalism grew out of feudalism, the economic structures that once existed under absolute monarchs.[4]

Modern capitalism was first described in the work of 18th-century Scottish philosopher Adam Smith. In Smith's book *An Inquiry into the Nature and Causes of the Wealth of Nations* (1776), he argues that capitalism works in everyone's interest. According to Smith, in a "free market," competition between sellers not only makes products affordable. The pursuit of profit also results in new ideas and well-planned, productive work. In other words, investment and competition drive economic progress.[5]

The concept of capitalism as we understand it today has existed since the 19th century. Western Europe is generally considered to be the birthplace of modern capitalism, although other parts of the world also had some of the economic features identified with it.

The motivation of self-interest

"It is not from the benevolence of the butcher, the brewer or the baker, that we expect our dinner, but from their regard to their own self interest. We address ourselves, not to their humanity but to their self-love, and never talk to them of our own necessities but of their advantages."[6]

Adam Smith

Scottish philosopher Adam Smith pioneered the study of economics in his book *An Inquiry into the Nature and Causes of the Wealth of Nations*. He believed that the "invisible hand" of a self-interested free market would create social order.

Socialism

Not everyone was happy with capitalism's transformation of social life. Repetitive, unskilled forms of labor such as factory work were the primary types of work. Some people feared that modern social life was based around economic production.

The biggest challenge to the ethics of capitalism came from socialism. Socialism is the economic theory that the means of production should be owned and operated by everyone. It began as a critique (criticism) of capitalism.[7]

Socialist ideology is most often associated with the writings of 19th-century German economist Karl Marx. Together with German historian Friedrich Engels, Marx drafted the **Communist** *Manifesto*. This is the central document of the economic theory that came to be known as **Marxism**.

According to the **Marxist** interpretation of history, capitalism creates economic inequalities between the rich and the poor. These differences prevent true political liberation. Marxism considers capitalism to be a stage, or step, in the evolution toward socialism.

A new social order

"[T]he final causes of all social changes and political revolutions are to be sought, not in men's brains, not in man's better insight in to eternal truth and justice, but in changes in the modes of production and exchange. They are sought, not in the philosophy, but in the economics of each particular epoch [era]. The growing perception that existing social institutions are unreasonable and unjust, that reason has become unreason, and right wrong, is only proof that in the modes of production and exchange changes have silently taken place with which the social order, adapted to earlier economic conditions, is no longer in keeping."[8]

—Friedrich Engels. In this quotation, Engels explains that social injustice can be generated by changes in economic conditions.

Marx wanted to create a society in which small communities would govern themselves. On a larger scale, he pictured a form of direct democracy in which citizens would send representatives to larger political units. But liberty cannot be achieved by voting alone. Within this political structure, everyone would own the means of production. The economy would be run for the benefit of the workers and society as a whole, rather than for private profit.[9]

German philosopher Karl Marx's economic and social theories inspired socialist movements all over the world.

The perfect society?

The desire for a just and fair society was expressed by many visionary political thinkers of the early 19th century. They imagined **utopias**, or perfect political systems in which social life was fulfilling and struggle did not exist. Some thinkers even went so far as to establish new communities based on these ideals.[10]

French reformer Henri de Saint-Simon emphasized the importance of education. He saw economic activity—primarily the development of resources—as the center of political life. In Saint-Simon's utopia, scientists and industrialists would lead society.[11]

French thinker Charles Fourier also considered work a necessary and vital activity. He believed people would find happiness through the freedom to choose their own form of work, which should involve both physical and mental activity. The work settlements he founded were intended to be starting points for social reform. But they soon failed.[12]

Welsh reformer Robert Owen believed that human nature is conditioned by surroundings. He felt that a good society would produce a good person. Owen managed successful mills (built at New Lanark in Scotland) using these principles. He treated his workers fairly and looked after their health and safety. Owen also experimented with building a utopian community in New Harmony, Indiana. It did not succeed.[13]

An empty prophecy

"Nearly all creators of Utopia have resembled the man who has a toothache, and therefore thinks happiness consists in not having a toothache. They wanted to produce a perfect society by an endless continuation of something that had only been valuable because it was temporary. The wider course would be to say that there are certain lines along which humanity must move, the grand strategy is mapped out, but detailed prophecy [predicting] is not our business. Whoever tries to imagine perfection simply reveals his own emptiness."[14]

British socialist George Orwell, author of the books *Nineteen Eighty-Four* and *Animal Farm*

Political thinkers and artists have imagined utopian societies that have been impossible to achieve in reality.

The fantasy of social order

Although these utopian thinkers did not achieve much in reality, their vision for a new way of life inspired later political thinkers to consider what kind of society they wanted to create. Their failed intentions also demonstrated the problem with trying to create a perfect model of society. Future political reformers learned to take political realities into account.

The early 20th century saw the rise of **totalitarian** governments, which attempted to control society on a large scale according to goals and ideals. As we will see in the next chapter, their pursuit of the ideal society at all costs had disastrous consequences.

TOTALITARIANISM

The democratic system was in crisis following World War I (1914–1918) and the worldwide economic Great Depression of the 1930s. When people were unhappy with the failures of democratic politics, this gave rise to **totalitarianism**. This is a system of rule based on a strong central government that controls all aspects of political and social life.[1]

In uncertain times, people looked for dramatic action and strong leadership to confront problems such as economic instability. In the postwar period, founders of totalitarian societies promised to change the world according to an ideal. Or, in countries where people felt unsettled by the rapid changes of the modern world, totalitarian leaders promised to prevent change. They aimed to restore the nation to the former glory of an idealized past.

Some political scientists consider totalitarianism a form of one-party democracy. This is because citizens typically put totalitarian regimes into power. Totalitarian governments present themselves as the sole democratic choice of the people. In the standard model, one party rules absolutely. It tolerates no political opposition or alternative political viewpoints. Loyalty to the regime is often encouraged through mass participation in public events and ceremonies.[2]

Mass events, such as this gymnastics display at the 65th anniversary of the founding of North Korea in 2010, create enthusiasm in totalitarian societies.

Ideology is power

In totalitarian governments, ideology is everything. Leaders use ideology to claim legitimacy. Totalitarian ideologies aim to create a new society based on grand ideals and goals.

An extreme tendency to conform, or try to fit in, is another totalitarian trait. Social life under totalitarian regimes is defined in terms of the citizen's duty to the state. The leading party dominates social life, making all social organizations extensions of political activity. Every citizen serves the party—and relies on party approval for social status. The ideal citizen is disciplined and obedient. Personal sacrifice for the greater good is seen as an important virtue.[3]

To achieve total power, ruling parties often identify political enemies and eliminate them. Totalitarian regimes use secret police organizations that operate outside of the law. These groups spy on citizens and restrict political opposition. Citizens can be arrested, detained, tortured, or relocated for criticizing the government. The shadowy existence of such organizations creates fear and suspicion among the population.[4]

Terror from within

"Totalitarianism is never content to rule by external means, namely, through the state and a machinery of violence; thanks to its peculiar ideology and the role assigned to it in this apparatus of coercion [forcing people to do something], totalitarianism has discovered a means of dominating and terrorizing human beings from within."[5]

–Hannah Arendt, *The Origins of Totalitarianism* (1951). In this work, German-American political theorist Arendt studied totalitarian systems and the social conditions that contributed to them. In this quotation, she explains how ideology can be used as a form of social control.

Totalitarian governments measure their success through various forms of social achievement. Military success is considered proof of national strength. Progress is also measured through goals of economic growth and modernization. Seemingly nonpolitical activities such as science and sports are also considered evidence of superiority.[6]

Benefits of totalitarianism?

Both **fascism** (see next page) and **communism** (see pages 38 to 41) are frequently described as totalitarian systems. The ethics and economies of each system in the early 20th century were radically different. But they were similar in many ways.[7] Both systems typically emphasized industrial growth, military spending, and self-sufficiency (freedom from having to trade with other countries).

These totalitarian governments did generate some rewards for their citizens. Citizens often mentioned a sense of self-worth that came from being involved in a grand social project. In addition, the party system offered chances for rapid social advancement. The guarantee of a job was a very important advantage, especially during the global Great Depression of the 1930s. Basic goods and welfare policies were also provided, which helped keep a solid living standard.[8]

At a Nazi Party rally in Nuremberg, Germany, in the late 1930s, the elite SS Guard gathers for a demonstration of discipline and unity.

The era of fascism

Fascism refers to a political movement that primarily developed in Italy, Germany, and Spain between the two world wars, roughly from 1922 to 1945.[9] **Fascist** governments were defined by aggressive nationalism (extreme national pride) and military strength.

Italian leader Benito Mussolini first introduced fascism in Italy. Following the success of Italian fascism, movements emerged in every major European country.[10] In Germany, fascism took on its most dominant form as the **Nazi**, or National Socialist, Party in 1933, led by Adolf Hitler.[11]

Fascism was a response to the changes in society, culture, and politics produced by World War I. As the basis for fascist ideology, ideals of nationalist unity and strength included elements of **racism**. In Nazi Germany, anti-Semitism (hatred of Jews) resulted in the worst **genocide** (mass killing) in modern history. Over 7 million people were killed, including Jews, people with different political views, homosexuals, and Roma. This has become known as the Holocaust.[12]

Many political scientists do not consider fascism a consistent political system. This is because there have been vast differences among specific fascist movements. What they have had in common are the violent oppression of political rivals and notions of nationalistic "purity." Fascist regimes have also cooperated with traditional political institutions such as the military, business interests, and the church. Different interpretations of fascism portray it in different ways. It can be viewed as a rapid mobilization of society, or as a desire to return to a simpler time.[13]

The ethical state

Mussolini rose to power by promoting the idea of an "ethical state." By this he meant a form of politics that would create noble, disciplined citizens according to a nationalistic ideal. Society's role was to promote the ethical and moral potential of every individual.[14] Should governments be concerned with trying to create ethical human beings? Can human nature be directed or controlled in a positive way by politics?

The legacy of fascism

World War II (1939–1945) marked the end of fascism as a political system. Fascist regimes were defeated and removed from power. The term fascism is still used today to describe certain political characteristics, such as the extreme enforcement of social order. It has also been applied to right-wing (conservative) terrorist groups and governments led by military dictators.

Fascism appeals to the longing for unity, safety, and community in the face of uncertainty. Given a significant crisis, fascism may someday reemerge. Economic instability may cause people to turn toward a charismatic leader who makes promises to improve their lives. Or people may seek to blame social problems on such factors as immigration or cultural differences. Whenever extreme nationalism gains wide appeal as a political solution, people run the risk of a return to a fascist type of government.[15]

Communism

Russia was another country in which a totalitarian government developed. In the early 20th century, Russian leader Vladimir Ilyich Lenin adapted Marxism. He helped form the ideas that inspired the Russian Bolsheviks. This was the revolutionary party that led the Russian Revolution in October 1917. A new form of socialist ideology arose out of the Russian Revolution and Lenin's ideas. This came to be widely known as communism.

The Bolsheviks found themselves fighting to preserve the progress of the revolution from elements that challenged it. At the same time, they had to defend the country itself from European powers during World War I. The need to fight a war on multiple fronts while beginning a program of rapid economic development increased the communist state's powers dramatically.[16] Eventually, Russia turned into the Soviet Union, a name given to a large area that included Russia and many territories from 1922 to 1991.

After Lenin died in 1924, General Secretary of the Communist Party Joseph Stalin rose in power. He finally grabbed control of the government in 1927. Stalin was a brutal ruler whose policies included the rapid transformation of the agriculture industry from 1928 to 1937, known as collectivization, which resulted in mass starvation, resettlement, and forced labor. It's estimated that over 10 million people died during this period as a result of collectivization. Stalin was also responsible for the notorious Great Purge of 1936 to 1938, in which around one million people considered political enemies were executed and millions more were banished to work camps known as gulags. Stalin continued to rule the Soviet Union until his death in 1953.[17]

Socialism in one state?

Marx's concept of socialism assumed that the establishment of a workers' state such as the Soviet Union would inspire a worldwide revolt of the working class. Marxists wanted this to happen especially in the West, where the working class was more developed.[18] However, the reality was quite different. Socialism failed to spread to the West, and Soviet communists tried to establish socialism in one state.

The Soviet form of communism therefore differed significantly from Marx's socialist ideals. According to Marx's theories, the state would gradually disappear as society progressed towards socialism. Instead, Soviet communism had a highly complicated and centralized state structure that was sometimes used to repress citizens or to force communism on other countries.

Propaganda posters like this one from the Soviet Union were often used by communist governments to inspire and motivate citizens. This Soviet poster from World War II tells soldiers to fight bravely and shows the figures of historic Russian military leaders in the background.

The spread of communism

Over time, communism did spread. After World War II, the Soviet empire began to include other countries in Eastern Europe and Asia. But communism often spread when the Soviet military established communist regimes in new countries. Because an outside military forced this change, these regimes often lacked a sense of legitimacy.[19]

Sometimes communist regimes came to power when local fighting forces fought to bring down the groups in power—for example, colonial rulers or corrupt regimes. This often happened in Latin America.

The decline of communism

In 1985, Mikhail Gorbachev became leader of the Communist Party in the Soviet Union. Gorbachev put in place policies that focused on a more practical application of socialist democracy. The policies, known as *glasnost* (openness), *perestroika* (economic restructuring), and *demokratsiya* (democratic accountability), were intended to bring the Soviet Union closer to Western democracy. They led to the fall of the Soviet Union between 1989 and 1991.[20] In communist countries that had been part of the Soviet Union, governments either reformed themselves or were removed by the organized protest of underground democratic groups.[21]

CHANGES IN CUBA

The island of Cuba, in the Caribbean, is home to one of the last remaining communist governments in the world. After a revolution overthrew the regime of Fulgencio Batista in 1959, revolutionary leader Fidel Castro became president. He would hold onto this role for 49 years.

The regime's stability allowed it to resist a United States–backed attempted coup in 1961. However, it has also resulted in a lack of political and economic progress. In 2008, Fidel Castro stepped down as president and his brother, Raúl, took over. In 2011, Raúl Castro proposed setting term limits of two five-year terms for politicians, in an attempt to refresh the political system with new ideas. As the revolutionaries themselves grow old, communism must adapt to a new era.[22]

The demilitarized zone (DMZ) between North and South Korea is the most heavily armed border in the world. It separates the communist North from the democratic South.

Today, many socialists agree that Soviet communism was not an accurate example of socialist goals. In fact, true socialism has not yet been realized.[23]

Totalitarianism today

Today, totalitarianism is considered a failed political system. Still, totalitarian traits can be found in some Latin American regimes and in the rule of dictators such as Kim Jong Il in North Korea until his death in 2011.[24]

People will always strive for simple solutions to political problems. They will also be vulnerable to the desire to conform and be influenced by strong political opinions. As long as these conditions exist, there is always the chance that totalitarianism will reemerge.[25]

COMPARING POLITICAL SYSTEMS

Political scientists often compare different forms of political organization. This can help to highlight some of the factors that shape policies in some governments. It can also predict the potential for change or reform in repressive states. Comparing political systems can also reveal ethical problems that all political systems share.

Nationalism

Nationalism, or pride in one's country or ethnic heritage, is a factor in every political system. It can often be a positive force. For example, nationalism can allow a nation to take down a repressive ruler. But nationalism can sometimes contain elements of racism, which leads to intolerance of other people. This can result in the denial of basic human rights.

At its most extreme, nationalism can also result in genocide, or ethnic cleansing. The Nazi Holocaust (see page 37) is the most famous example. But, unfortunately, there have been other instances of this type of nationalism during the 20th century.[1]

Yugoslavia, in southeastern Europe, broke down under ethnic tensions in the 1990s. People there broke off to form their own states. Serbian nationalists performed ethnic cleansing, which is the mass killing of members of an ethnic group. One example of this included the July 1995 massacre of nearly 8,000 Muslims, mostly men and boys, near the town of Srebrenica in Bosnia.[2]

In Rwanda, in central and eastern Africa, there were also ethnic tensions and nationalist feelings. This led to the group of people known as Hutus slaughtering approximately 800,000 people known as Tutsis. This happened over 100 days in 1994.[3]

Corruption

When people abuse positions of power or resources for private benefit, this is called corruption. It is another common problem in every political system. No society is free of corruption. It occurs in both advanced and developing countries.

When governments must answer to the people, this eliminates some corruption. Honest political processes also help. But democracy does not always offer enough protection from corruption. For example, democratic governments often do business with or otherwise support corrupt regimes if it benefits them in some way.

In terms of ethics, corruption damages politics. When people can abuse positions of power, this weakens political competition and participation. People lose interest in the political process when they become disgusted by too much corruption.[4]

Here, experts from the International War Crimes Tribunal investigate a mass grave of some of the victims of the Srebrenica massacre.

Mixed systems

In reality, no political system exists in pure form. Most governments cannot be easily defined as one system. In fact, governments often combine elements of different systems. For example, the Islamic Republic of Iran contains elements of democracy—but within a theocratic framework (see pages 14 and 15).

The United States is mostly a liberal capitalist democracy. However, it has many socialist institutions, such as the postal service and public education. Programs such as Social Security (money paid to people after they retire), unemployment insurance (money paid for a time after people lose their jobs), and Medicare (health insurance for people over 65, among others) are also socialist.[5]

In some governments, the constitution allows the executive (for example, the president) to assume authoritarian powers in the event of an emergency or crisis. Such authority, although dangerous to everyday personal liberties, can be helpful in extreme situations such as war or natural disaster.

Some political scientists consider this balance of different systems necessary to successful government. Aspects of different systems are suited to particular political or social purposes. Governments can adapt the weaknesses of individual systems in response to different challenges.

"ONE COUNTRY, TWO SYSTEMS"

In the early 1980s, China had a "reunification policy." It allowed capitalist economic and political systems to exist in the independent regions of Hong Kong, Macau, and Taiwan. These existed alongside China's socialist system. The policy, known as "one country, two systems," was promoted by Communist Party leader and economic reformer Deng Xiaoping. Today, China itself has added many capitalistic elements into its socialist economy.[6]

Iran's president Mahmoud Ahmadinejad gives a speech in front of a poster of Iran's founder Ayatollah Ruhollah Khomeini in 2011. In the Islamic Republic of Iran, elected political leaders share power with religious leaders, such as Ayatollahs (Islamic clerics).

A historical example

The Arab Spring uprisings of 2011 (see pages 4 and 5) were the most significant democratic revolutions since the end of the Soviet Union in 1989. While it is too early to know what the long-term effects will be, we can look to history for examples of successful, positive transitions. One such example is Czechoslovakia's transformation from totalitarian communism to a democratic republic (see box at right).

Czech protesters surround Soviet tanks in August 1968. The Soviet Union invaded Czechoslovakia to end a series of democratic reforms by Czech leader Alexander Dubcek. The brief period of political freedom was known as the Prague Spring.

CHARTER 77 AND THE VELVET REVOLUTION

In 1976, communist police in Czechoslovakia, in central Europe, arrested members of a rock band called the Plastic People of the Universe. They were charged with "disturbing the peace" because they had long hair, wore unusual clothes, and sang loud, angry songs.

In response to the arrest, a group of activists issued a statement in January 1977 known as "Charter 77." In it, the group demanded that the government respect human rights. Playwright Václav Havel, a founder of the group, called the arrest of the Plastic People "an attack by the totalitarian system on life itself, on the very essence of human freedom."[7]

Charter 77 activists were targeted and harassed by communist authorities. Many were forced out of their jobs. Several, including Havel, were imprisoned. Operating in secret, Charter 77 remained active throughout the 1980s, continuing to call the world's attention to human rights abuses in Czechoslovakia. Although the alternative policies they proposed were ignored by the communist regime, Charter 77 maintained the ideas of democratic opposition and freedom of thought. These ideas paved the way for the end of communist control of the government.[8]

When peaceful student protestors were violently attacked by police in November 1989, many Czech citizens turned against the communist regime. Charter 77 members helped organize Civic Forum. This group led the transition from communism to a more open, democratic system.[9] The victory became known as the Velvet Revolution because of its peaceful nature. It showed that democratic institutions need to be in place to make the transition from an oppressive government to a more open society.

In December 1989, Havel was selected to be president, a position he held through 1992, when Czechoslovakia split into the Czech Republic and Slovakia. He then served as the first president of the Czech Republic from 1993 to 2003. He remained for many a symbol of democratic hope and the defense of human rights.[10]

WORLD SYSTEMS

Political problems often extend beyond governments to include international relations. The governments of the world must respect international treaties (agreements) and political alliances (groups formed for mutual benefit) such as the European Union and the United Nations.

If most countries in the world recognize a standard of human rights, this makes it hard for repressive regimes to get away with human rights abuses. If countries express concern about the development of nuclear weapons, this, too, makes it difficult for a regime to develop them without consequences.

International organizations can make governments responsible for their actions. In July 2011, the European Court of Human Rights made an important ruling about the United Kingdom's role in the 2003 invasion of Iraq. The court said that the United Kingdom's involvement in the war made it responsible for failing to investigate the killing of Iraqi civilians by British soldiers. According to the court, as an occupying force in Iraq, the UK and U.S. assumed "the exercise of some of the public powers normally to be exercised by a sovereign [independent] government." The ruling set a standard. It established that European governments can be judged on their human rights record beyond what happens within their borders. They can also be judged according to how their military operates in foreign states.[1]

NATO INTERVENTION IN KOSOVO

When Serbian president Slobodan Milosevic's police forces massacred citizens in the province of Kosovo in January 1999, the international community went on alert. Milosevic had been forcing ethnic Albanians to leave Kosovo for years, using methods that grew more and more violent over time. The North Atlantic Treaty Organization (NATO), an international military alliance, decided to intervene. Starting in March, NATO led air strikes against Milosevic's forces to put an end to the violent repression and ethnic cleansing. The bombings were controversial, as they affected both civilian and military targets and also bypassed the authorization of the United Nations Security Council. In June, Milosevic agreed to remove his forces from Kosovo. NATO peacekeepers stayed on to protect the population. Kosovo finally gained full independence from Serbia by becoming a separate nation on February 17, 2008.[2]

U.S. president Barack Obama delivers a speech to the United Nations General Assembly in 2010. The United Nations is an organization for international dialogue, although it also issues resolutions, conducts studies, and sponsors international humanitarian missions.

The **International Criminal Court (ICC)** in The Hague, in the Netherlands, is another authority on international justice and human rights. It was set up in 2002. The first international criminal court at The Hague was set up following World War II to try Nazi war criminals.

The ICC issues arrest warrants for world leaders judged guilty of human rights abuses, such as attacks against their own citizens. The ICC does not have a police force to enforce its warrants. However, a warrant limits the guilty party's ability to travel internationally and makes prosecution easier when leaders are overthrown or exiled. Some world leaders who have been tried for war crimes by international criminal courts include Charles G. Taylor of Liberia (in west Africa) and Slobodan Milosevic of Serbia (in the former Yugoslavia).[3]

International groups have also organized to bring attention to the issue of corruption. Hong Kong's Independent Commission Against Corruption has become the model for similar agencies established around the world, including Transparency International in Berlin, Germany. The Organization for Economic Co-Operation and Development negotiated an anti-bribery treaty. This protects developing countries from the influence of wealthy nations.[4]

International economic systems

In modern times, global economic systems have gained a lot of influence over the politics of individual countries. The capitalist system has produced much dissent. When global stock markets go up and down, this has results that affect people. It can lead to inequality and unemployment.

The spread of nuclear weapons is another major concern for the international community. Eight states have openly developed and tested nuclear weapons: The United States, the United Kingdom, France, China, Russia, India, Pakistan, and North Korea. Israel is also suspected to have nuclear weapons. Other states may have developed them in secret, and international terrorist groups have expressed a determination to acquire them. The aggressive use of nuclear weapons would be disastrous for life on our planet, which puts enormous pressure on international cooperation to avoid any kind of nuclear confrontation.

Antiglobalization activists in Bern, Switzerland, protest the meeting of the World Economic Forum in 2008.

The international network of political, cultural, and economic connections between states is known as globalization. More specifically, globalization refers to the economic interconnectedness of international financial markets. Large companies, called corporations, also influence worldwide realities. Multinational corporations are companies that operate in many countries. These companies often "outsource" labor to the countries with the lowest labor costs and protections for workers.[5]

Perhaps the biggest issues to cross national borders are environmental threats. Pollution, oil spills, global warming, and other problems are concerns for all nations. These problems have the potential to cause catastrophic damage to the entire planet.[6]

GLOBAL FINANCIAL PROTESTS

On October 15, 2011, protests against the global financial systems broke out in cities around the world, including New York, London, Rome, and Tokyo. The protests were largely inspired by the Occupy Wall Street movement, a protest that began in New York on September 17, 2011, and quickly spread to cities all over the United States.

While the protesters had a variety of complaints, they were mainly organized in opposition to the failures of the global banking system. Many were still reeling from the effects of a world-wide economic recession (downturn) that began in December of 2007.

The recession was linked to multiple causes, including international debt and corrupt investment practices. While major financial institutions that had taken on risky investments were rescued by government intervention, the recession caused many people to lose their homes or their jobs.

Inequality between the rich and the poor also continued to grow in many countries. In Berlin, a German protester told the New York Times, "I have no problem with capitalism, but I find the way the financial system is functioning deeply unethical. We shouldn't bail out the banks. We should bail out the people."[7]

CHANGING THE WORLD

The protest movement that overthrew Tunisia's dictator set an example that sparked the Arab Spring protests (see pages 4 and 5). Tunisia was also the first of the newly liberated Arab Spring countries to hold a free election.

On October 25, 2011, Tunisians voted for a national assembly to draft a new constitution, pick a prime minister, and govern the country. Ennahda, a moderate Islamic party, won nearly half the vote, while the rest went to other nonreligious parties such as Congress for the Republic and Democratic Forum for Labor and Liberties.

Tunisians had many different opinions about the election result. Protesters who feared a theocratic government alleged election fraud. Some considered Ennahda the symbol of a history of opposition to the previous dictatorship and a chance for change. Representatives of other political parties saw the result as a chance for cooperation between Islamic and nonreligious political parties, and an expression of the desire of voters to avoid a civil war. Whether Tunisia can balance religious authority and political freedom will be seen in the years to come.

But what does this mean for the other newly liberated countries in the region? What will happen in Egypt or Libya? Every country is shaped by its own history and political traditions, but events such as Tunisia's election can still serve as an instructive example of the possibilities and dangers of establishing a new government.

The future of political systems

The history of modern political systems is largely a global evolution toward democracy. Democratic systems are generally regarded as the most legitimate and ethically fair form of government. Still, democratic systems present a wide variety of issues that concern political scientists. Leaving political responsibility to professional politicians means that those politicians may lose touch with the concerns of everyday citizens and devote their energy instead to re-election strategies that keep them in office. They may also avoid taking a stand on controversial issues if they think it may harm their careers. This can sometimes prevent governments from developing effective policies, which in turn causes citizens to lose trust in their elected officials.

Workers gather on May Day (May 1), 2010, in San Salvador, the capital of El Salvador, in Central America. May Day is celebrated around the world as a workers' holiday. It is seen as an opportunity for mass political protest.

Nationalism is still a powerful force in the world as well, particularly in times of economic or political crisis. There is always a danger of a return to systems that seem to offer a solution to world problems. This may mean the emergence of a new form of fascism, possibly based on religious extremism, or communist totalitarianism.

Whatever the future holds, it is important to consider the historical successes and failures of political systems. Understanding the past will help as we strive to develop even more ethical systems of politics.

How can you shape your political system?

Find out who your political representatives are and how they vote about issues that are important to you. If you disagree, write them a letter to tell them what you think.

IMAGINING DYSTOPIA

Literature has often explored fictional political systems. This is a useful way to examine existing forms of government. This genre, or literary style, is known as dystopian fiction.

Dystopia, which means "bad place" in Greek, is a dark reflection of utopia. Dystopian novels describe ethically flawed systems of politics. Often these systems present themselves as utopian.

Writers create imaginary dystopias to exaggerate and highlight unethical methods of social control. They also hope to warn of the dangers of questionable political ideals. These novels are often meant to encourage a greater sense of political awareness. The following are some of the best-known dystopian novels.

Brave New World

In Aldous Huxley's *Brave New World* (1932), world peace has been achieved—but at a cost. A totalitarian World State has engineered a peaceful society by limiting the population. Social and economic stability are also achieved through problematic means. The state supports extreme consumerism, or the desire to buy things. It also has people use a drug called soma. In a society where individuality is considered antisocial, everyone is conditioned to be happy. A young man raised as a "savage" outside the boundaries of the Brave New World must confront its conformity in this novel.

Nineteen Eighty-Four

In George Orwell's *Nineteen Eighty-Four* (1949), there is a society based on constant war, constant surveillance (watching people), and the manipulation of history. Winston Smith, a civil servant, sets on a path of rebellion against the totalitarian Party and its figurehead, Big Brother. Orwell's classic dystopian novel explores themes such as language as a form of mind control.

Fahrenheit 451

In Ray Bradbury's *Fahrenheit 451* (1951), the United States has become an anti-intellectual, pleasure-hungry country. Reading has become a crime. A firefighter given the task of burning books accidentally discovers their value. He struggles to preserve the importance of memory as part of human experience.

Player Piano

Kurt Vonnegut's *Player Piano* (1952) describes a modernized future in which machines run society. This makes human beings useless. The revolutionary Ghost Shirt organization offers humans the chance to recover their sense of purpose through political action.

Vonnegut also wrote a number of dystopian short stories, including "Harrison Bergeron" (1961). This story takes the democratic ideal of equality to extremes. A future government imposes limitations on individual abilities, so that everyone is only as capable as society's weakest member.

Dystopian books and films, such as Fritz Lang's *Metropolis* (1927), are often set in the future and have elements of science fiction. However, they are mostly concerned with the possible negative effects of existing political and social problems.

The Handmaid's Tale

In Margaret Atwood's *The Handmaid's Tale* (1985), the former United States, known as the Republic of Gilead, is a totalitarian theocracy. It has stripped women of their rights, making them reproductive slaves. Seen through the eyes of a female slave, the novel depicts a frightening society based on sexual and racial division.

Cloud Atlas

David Mitchell's *Cloud Atlas* (2004) tells of a capitalist totalitarian future. A female clone who was engineered to serve fast food attempts to rebel against her social status and the expectations of a hyper-capitalist society. The theme of repressed political identity is also echoed throughout the other layers of Mitchell's novel.

GLOSSARY

absolute power total control of political and social life

Arab person from an ethnic and cultural group located primarily in North Africa and the Middle East

authoritarian political system based on a strong central authority that governs in its own self-interest

capitalism economic system based on the production of goods for a profit and the private ownership of property and wealth

capitalist relating to an economic system based on the private ownership of resources

civilian anyone who is not a member of the armed forces

colonial relating to a system of rule in which a state extends its power and authority over other territories

communism political and economic system developed from Marxism, in which all areas of the economy including the means of production, business, media, and farming are owned and operated by the state

communist relating to an economic system based on government ownership of resources

constitution official framework of rules that defines the function of government in relation to the rights of individuals

constitutional monarchy form of monarchy in which the monarch's power is limited by a formal set of rules

corrupt dishonest or unethical

corruption abuse of a position of power for private advantage

coup sudden action to gain power

democracy government chosen by the people

democratic characterized by political equality

dictator ruler with absolute power

dystopia style of fiction that criticizes so-called utopian political solutions; the term is also used to refer to a bad or oppressive political system

economic refers to the production and distribution of goods and services

Enlightenment period of philosophical and cultural advancement in Europe during the mid-17th and 18th centuries

ethical relating to moral standards of what is good or right

ethics concepts of right and wrong as they relate to human behavior

ethnic characteristic of a group or nation that shares a cultural tradition

fascism totalitarian political system based on aggressive nationalism and military strength

fascist relating to a totalitarian political system based on nationalism and military power, especially the conservative regimes that arose in Western Europe prior to World War II; also used to describe the excessive enforcement of social order

genocide deliberate mass killing of a racial group

ideology system of thought about how people should live

institution organization devoted to the promotion of a program

International Criminal Court (ICC) authority on international justice and human rights

legitimacy in politics, the acceptance of authority or systems of rule

Marxism system of thought developed by Karl Marx that interprets capitalism as a step in the struggle for socialism

Marxist relating to the economic theories of Karl Marx

monarch absolute ruler of a state, such as a king or emperor

monarchy rule by a king or queen, typically inherited through birth

nation group of people united by culture, ethnicity, or political identity

nationalism extreme devotion to one's own nation

Nazi fascist National Socialist Party that ruled Germany from 1933 to 1945

oligarchy government by an elite group

parliament national law-making assembly

pluralism competing political views

policy procedure or plan of action regarding a certain issue

political concerned with public affairs, such as matters of state or government

political scientist person who studies political systems

politics process by which human beings organize social life

racism intolerance and hatred of different races

reform political change

regime system of government loyal to the ruler

repressive limiting through violence or force

republic state in which the head of government is chosen by the people or their representatives

right ethical or moral guarantee, considered the basis for justice and equality

socialism system of economic and political thought that aspires to a classless society in which everyone owns the means of production

socialist relating to an economic system based on the collective social ownership of resources

state independent political territory

theocracy rule by religious authority

theocratic relating to a form of rule by religious authority

totalitarian relating to central government control of all aspects of political and social life

totalitarianism system of rule based on a strong central government that controls all aspects of political and social life

utopia ideal society or place

NOTES ON SOURCES

The Arab Spring Revolt (pp. 4–5)

1. Bob Simon, "How a Slap Sparked Tunisia's Revolution," *60 Minutes*, CBS, February 20, 2011, http://www.cbsnews.com/stories/2011/02/20/60minutes/main20033404.shtml.
2. Ibid.
3. Garry Blight and Sheila Pulham, "Arab Spring: An Interactive Timeline of Middle East Protests," The *Guardian*, July 12, 2011, http://www.guardian.co.uk/world/interactive/2011/mar/22/middle-east-protest-interactive-timeline.
4. Chris McGreal and Jack Shenker, "Hosni Mubarak Resigns and Egypt Celebrates a New Dawn," The *Guardian*, February 11, 2011, http://www.guardian.co.uk/world/2011/feb/11/hosni-mubarak-resigns-egypt-cairo.

What Are Political Systems? (pp. 6–9)

1. Jacob Ben-Amittay, *The History of Political Thought* (New York: Philosophical Library, 1972), 3.
2. Ibid., 4.
3. J. Denis Derbyshire and Ian Derbyshire, *Political Systems of the World* (Oxford: Helicon Publishing Ltd., 1996), 3.
4. Ibid., 23.
5. David Held, "Democracy," in *The Oxford Companion to Politics of the World*, ed. Joel Krieger (New York: Oxford University Press, 2001), 198.

Authoritarianism (pp. 10–17)

1. John F. Burns, "NATO Begins Helicopter Attacks in Hopes of Ending the Stalemate With Qaddafi," The *New York Times*, June 4, 2011, http://www.nytimes.com/2011/06/05/world/africa/05libya.html.
2. Juan J. Linz, "Authoritarianism," in *Oxford Companion to Politics*, 57.
3. Ibid.
4. Aidan Lewis, "Profile: Muammar Gaddafi," *BBC News*, June 27, 2011, http://www.bbc.co.uk/news/world-africa-12488278; John F. Burns, "New Questions in Lockerbie Bomber's Release," The *New York Times*, August 21, 2009, http://www.nytimes.com/2009/08/22/world/europe/22lockerbie.html.
5. Linz, "Authoritarianism," 61.
6. Derbyshire and Derbyshire, *Political Systems of the World*, 34.
7. Ibid., 32.
8. Ibid., 353.
9. Andrew Heywood, *Political Ideologies: An Introduction* (New York: St. Martin's Press, 1992), 29.
10. P. J. Taylor, ed., *World Government* (New York: Oxford University Press, 1990), 86–87.
11. Linz, "Authoritarianism," 58.

12. Derbyshire and Derbyshire, *Political Systems of the World*, 34.

13. Ibid., 35.

14. Owen Bennett Jones, *Pakistan: Eye of the Storm*, (New Haven and London: Yale University Press, 2009), 25–29.

15. Derbyshire and Derbyshire, *Political Systems of the World*, 36.

16. Ibid., 32.

17. Nadim Audi, "Offering Slow, Small Changes, Morocco's King Stays in Power," The *New York Times*, July 10, 2011, http://www.nytimes.com/2011/07/11/world/africa/11morocco.html.

Democracy (pp. 18–25)

1. Derbyshire and Derbyshire, *Political Systems of the World*, 24.

2. Ibid., 25.

3. Held, "Democracy," 199.

4. Seth Mydans and Thomas Fuller, "Thais Back Ousted Prime Minister's Party," The *New York Times*, July 2, 2011, http://www.nytimes.com/2011/07/04/world/asia/04thailand.html.

5. Derbyshire and Derbyshire, *Political Systems of the World*, 36.

6. Ibid., 24.

7. Held, "Democracy," 196.

8. Ben-Amittay, *History of Political Thought*, 245.

9. Held, "Democracy," 196–97.

10. Ibid., 199.

11. Ibid., 197.

12. Derbyshire and Derbyshire, *Political Systems of the World*, 511–12.

13. Held, "Democracy," 197.

14. Ibid., 196.

15. Ibid., 198.

16. Ibid.

17. Ibid., 196.

18. Derbyshire and Derbyshire, *Political Systems of the World*, 26.

19. Seth Mydans and Liz Robbins, "Burmese Dissident Is Freed After Long Detention," The *New York Times*, November 13, 2010, http://www.nytimes.com/2010/11/14/world/asia/14myanmar.html; Ellen Nakashima, "Burma's Iron 'Aunty,'" The *Washington Post*, October 13, 2003, http://www.washingtonpost.com/ac2/wp-dyn?pagename=article&contentId=A18107-2003Oct12.

20. Held, "Democracy," 200.

21. Pratap Mehta, "India," in *Oxford Companion to Politics*, 387; The *New York Times*, "India," Times Topics, http://topics.nytimes.com/top/news/international/countriesandterritories/india/index.html.

Economic Alternatives (pp. 26–33)

1. Meghnad Desai, "Capitalism," in *Oxford Companion to Politics*, 108.

2. Ibid.

3. Ibid.

4. Ibid.

5. "Adam Smith," *The Concise Encyclopedia of Economics*, www.econlib.org/library/Enc/bios/Smith.html; www.adamsmith.org/adam-smith/.

6. Adam Smith, *An Inquiry into the Nature and Causes of the Wealth of Nations*, 1776; www.econlib.org/library/Smith/smWN1.html.

7. Desai, "Capitalism," 109.

8. Friedrich Engels, "Socialism: Utopian and Scientific," in *Marxism: Essential Writings*, ed. David McLellan (New York: Oxford University Press, 1988), 63.

9. Held, "Democracy," 199.

10. Ben-Amittay, *History of Political Thought*, 269.

11. Ibid., 269–70.

12. Ibid., 270–71.

13. Ibid., 271–72.

14. George Orwell, "Why Socialists Don't Believe in Fun," *Tribune*, December 20, 1943, http://www.k-1.com/Orwell/site/work/essays/fun.html.

Totalitarianism (pp. 34–41)

1. Linz, "Authoritarianism," 58.

2. Alfred G. Meyer, "Totalitarianism," in *Oxford Companion to Politics*, 916.

3. Ibid.

4. Ibid.

5. Hannah Arendt, *The Origins of Totalitarianism* (New York: Schocken Books, 2004), 431.

6. Alfred G. Meyer, "Totalitarianism," in *Oxford Companion to Politics*, 916.

7. Meyer, "Totalitarianism," 916.

8. Ibid., 916–17.

9. Claudio G. Segrè, "Fascism," in *Oxford Companion to Politics*, 274.

10. Ibid., 275.

11. Ibid.

12. Ibid., 274.

13. Ibid., 276.

14. Ibid., 275.

15. Ibid., 276.

16. Derbyshire and Derbyshire, *Political Systems of the World*, 29.

17. Bill Keller, "Major Soviet Paper Says 20 Million Died As Victims of Stalin," The *New York Times*, February 4, 1989, www.nytimes.com/1989/02/04/world/major-soviet-paper-says-20-million-died-as-victims-of-stalin.html.

18. Derbyshire and Derbyshire, *Political Systems of the World*, 313–314.

19. Ibid.

20. Ibid., 32.

21. Meyer, "Totalitarianism," 917.

22. Randal C. Archibold, "Cuban Leader Proposes Term Limits in Sign of New Era," The *New York Times*, April 16, 2011, http://www.nytimes.com/2011/04/17/world/americas/17cuba.html.

23. Derbyshire and Derbyshire, *Political Systems of the World*, 29.

24. Meyer, "Totalitarianism," 917.

25. Ibid.

Comparing Political Systems (pp. 42–47)

1. Derbyshire and Derbyshire, *Political Systems of the World*, 33.

2. Marlise Simons, "Court Declares Bosnia Killings Were Genocide," The *New York Times*, February 27, 2007, www.nytimes.com/2007/02/27/world/europe/27hague.html.

3. "Genocide in Rwanda," United Human Rights Council, www.unitedhumanrights.org/genocide/genocide_in_rwanda.htm; "Rwanda: How the genocide happened," *BBC News*: Africa, December 18, 2008, http://news.bbc.co.uk/2/hi/1288230.stm.

4. Michael Johnston, "Corruption," in *Oxford Companion to Politics*, 177.

5. Meyer, "Totalitarianism," 917.

6. Wen Qing, "One Country, Two Systems: The Best Way to Peaceful Reunification," *Beijing Review*, May 26, 2009; www.bjreview.com.cn/nation/txt/2009-05/26/content_197568.htm.

7. Dan Bilefsky, "Czechs' Velvet Revolution Paved by Plastic People," The *New York Times*, November 15, 2009, http://www.nytimes.com/2009/11/16/world/europe/16iht-czech.html.

8. Sharon L. Wolchik, "Charter 77," in *Oxford Companion to Politics*, 123–24.

9. Sharon L. Wolchik, "Charter 77," in *Oxford Companion to Politics*, 123–24.

10. Sharon L. Wolchik, "Havel, Václav," in *Oxford Companion to Politics*, 352–53.

World Systems (pp. 48–51)

1. Owen Bowcott, "Iraq Abuse Ruling by European Court Says UK Failed Human Rights Role," The *Guardian*, July 7, 2011, http://www.guardian.co.uk/world/2011/jul/07/iraq-abuse-european-court-ruling.

2. "Kosovo," The *New York Times*: TimesTopics, July 23, 2010, topics.nytimes.com/top/news/international/countriesandterritories/serbia/kosovo/index.html.

3. Marlise Simons, "Charges of War Crimes Brought Against Qaddafi," The *New York Times*, June 27, 2011, http://www.nytimes.com/2011/06/28/world/africa/28libya.html.

4. Johnston, "Corruption," 178.

5. David Held and Anthony McGrew, "Globalization," in *The Oxford Companion to Politics of the World*, ed. Joel Krieger (New York: Oxford University Press, 2001), 324–327.

6. Nazli Choucri, "Environmentalism," in *The Oxford Companion to Politics of the World*, ed. Joel Krieger (New York: Oxford University Press, 2001), 353–255.

7. Carla Buckley and Rachel Donadio, "Buoyed by Wall St. Protests, Rallies Sweep the Globe," The *New York Times*, October 15, 2011, www.nytimes.com/2011/10/16/world/occupy-wall-street-protests-worldwide.html.

FIND OUT MORE

Books

Baylis, John, Steve Smith, and Patricia Owens. *The Globalization of World Politics: An Introduction to International Relations*. New York: Oxford University Press, 2011.

The Book of Rule: How the World Is Governed. New York: Dorling Kindersley, 2004.

Downing, David, and Richard Tames. *Political and Economic Systems* (series). Chicago: Heinemann Library, 2008.

Krieger, Joel, ed. *The Oxford Companion to Politics of the World*. New York: Oxford University Press, 2003.

Minogue, Kenneth. *Politics: A Very Short Introduction*. New York: Oxford University Press, 2000.

Segal Block, Marta. *Tunisia* (Countries Around the World series). Chicago: Heinemann Library, 2012.

DVDs

The Battle of Algiers (1966)
Director Gillo Pontecorvo's classic war movie was filmed not long after a 1962 revolution overthrew French rule in the African country of Algeria. It reconstructs the brutal tactics of both the French forces and the Algerian independence fighters, some of whom appear in the film.

Che (2008)
Director Steven Soderbergh's two-part epic biography of revolutionary Che Guevara contrasts the success of the Cuban revolution with the failure to export revolution to the South American country of Bolivia.

Chicago 10 (2007)

This documentary focuses on the political theater of the protests against the U.S. government during the 1968 Democratic National Convention in Chicago. The story is told half in documentary footage, and half in an animated reenactment of the famous trial of the protest leaders.

Reds (1981)

Warren Beatty directs and stars in this drama about John Reed, the U.S. reporter who covered the 1917 Russian Revolution. Although he supported the revolution, Reed later became disillusioned by communist politics.

The Wind That Shakes the Barley (2006)

This story is about two brothers living during the early 1920s Irish independence movement as Ireland struggled to be free of Great Britain. The film depicts the struggle between different tactics for political change. Director Ken Loach's films are well known for their political realism.

Websites

There are many news websites that cover politics, including the following:

www.cnn.com/POLITICS

This website carries the news network CNN's top political stories.

www.nytimes.com/pages/politics/index.html

Read top political news from The *New York Times* here.

www.worldpress.org

This site features news gathered from different sources from around the world.

www.icc-cpi.int/Menus/ICC

Explore this website to learn more about the International Criminal Court.

INDEX